A PRIMER ON THEOLOGICAL RESEARCH TOOLS

R. A. Krupp

UNIVERSITY
PRESS OF
AMERICA

Lanham • New York • London

Copyright © 1990 by

University Press of America,® Inc.

4720 Boston Way
Lanham, MD 20706

3 Henrietta Street
London WC2E 8LU England

British Cataloging in Publication Information Available

Library of Congress Cataloging-in-Publication Data

Krupp, Robert Allen.
A primer on theological research tools / R.A. Krupp.
p.   cm.
1. Theology—Research.   2. Theology—Bibliography.   I. Title.
BR118.K7   1990   291.2'072—dc20   89–14617 CIP

ISBN 0–8191–7519–6 (alk. paper)

To Collette

A Primer on Theological Research Tools

Preface

PREFACE

What follows is an introductory text that has arisen out of the author's experience teaching research methods at Western Seminary, in Portland, Oregon. It is designed to build skills in two areas. The first is the ability to evaluate the seemingly endless stream of reference tools put on the market for the theological student, the pastor, and the teacher in theological studies. The second aim is to develop skills in the use of these tools to find factual information or bibliographic citations.

There are three possible goals for studying research skills. One would be to develop writing skills for the effective communication of the fruit of one's research. A second would be to further one's grasp of research theory. This is foundational to preparing and presenting the fruit of one's study. This book addresses neither of these worthy goals. It seeks to meet a more basic need. It addresses a need faced by every student, every teacher, everyone who seeks to answer questions in religious studies. They each need to be able to use basic reference tools to find facts and bibliographic citations quickly and accurately.

The approach is unashamedly interactive. Research skills embrace both art and science. Practice perfects the skills needed for success in this area. While answering the questions in this primer, students will develop a strategy for theological research. They will also develop a grid for evaluating new tools which will come on the market during the course of their ministry. The choice of tools in this book does not aim to be exhaustive. It aims rather to give the student samples of the various genres of reference works. The tools examined in this course of study are not limited to those that the student would buy. Included are books clearly beyond the financial resources of most students. It is hoped that during the course of this study the student will become acquainted with the tools available and formulate a strategy for both personal book purchase and regular library use of more exotic reference materials.

Works whose scope will not be duplicated in this primer and whose insights supplement this volume include Richard E. Davies, <u>Handbook for Doctor of Ministry Projects</u> (University Press of America, 1984), Robert J. Kepple, <u>Reference Works for Theological Research</u> (University Press of America, 1981) and Cyril J. Barber, <u>Introduction to Theological Research</u> (Moody Press, 1982).

A note of thanks should be given to Professor Thomas Slavens. It was as his Research Assistant that the author first encountered this methodology of instruction so effectively used by him in courses at the University of Michigan, School of Information and Library Studies in Ann Arbor. It is hoped that this small effort to apply the principles that have guided Professor Slavens' teaching will aid seminarians and other students in theological studies. It is the author's desire that the exercises will serve students in the preparation for and fulfilling of their ministries.

Two people deserve particular thanks for their work in the preparation of this volume. Mrs. Bonnie Liljenberg, my Executive Secretary as I serve as Vice President for Administration at Western Seminary, has saved the author from many mistakes by her editing. The ones that remain are mine. Mrs. Lori Einfalt who was my secretary during the early phases of writing and testing questions for this primer gave many hours toward its success. Without their aid this project would not have been completed.

LESSON 1- GENERAL REFERENCE TOOLS

Adams, Charles Joseph, ed., A Reader's Guide to the
     Great Religions. 2d. ed., New York: Free Press,
     1977.

Barber, Cyril J. The Minister's Library. Grand Rapids:
     Baker Book House. 1974. 2 vols. with supplements.

Wilson, John F. and Thomas P. Slavens. Research Guide
     to Religious Studies. Chicago: American Library
     Association, 1982.

The works considered in this introductory unit serve as
general introductions to theological research. They
contain annotated bibliographies, bibliographic essays,
and other aids in evaluating reference tools.

The work by Slavens and Wilson has two parts. Part one,
written by John F. Wilson, is an introductory essay on
religious scholarship. It contains references to key
works and bibliographies of important reference sources.
The second part, constructed under the directorship of
Thomas Slavens, is a subject oriented annotated
bibliography of reference tools in religious studies.
The first section of this part, beginning on page 107,
lists general works divided by type of tool. Sections
follow covering mysticism, sacred books, and reference
tools for particular religions. The longest section is
that for Christianity.   The work concludes with
author-title and subject indices. Read a section of the
introductory essay to ascertain the scope and level of
treatment of Wilson's work and then begin looking at
various annotations. Answer the following questions in
order to ascertain the peculiarities of this work:

1.   Who is the author of the Dictionary of Religious
     Terms?

1

2.   In what year was <u>A Bibliography of New Testament Bibliographies</u> published by Seabury?

3.   Who is the author of <u>Saints and Their Attributes, With a Guide to Localities and Patronage</u>?

4.   In what year was Fluk's work, <u>Jews in the Soviet Union</u>, published?

5.   Into what sections is Ofori's work on African religions divided?

6.   Is there an index to titles in the <u>Bibliography on Buddhism</u> by Shinsho Hanayama?

7.   To what work is <u>Encyclopedic Dictionary of Judaica</u> intended to be a companion?

8.   What is the difference in emphasis between the <u>American Jewish Yearbook</u>, and <u>Jewish Yearbook: An Annual Record of Matters Jewish</u>?

9.   Which work has more pages, Mead's <u>Encyclopedia of Religious Quotations</u>, or Woods' <u>The World Treasury of Religious Quotations</u>?

10. Find a dictionary of mythology which contains the mythologies of India, China, Japan, Siberia, and Africa, as well as Celtic and Germanic mythologies.

11. Who is the publisher of <u>Religion Index One</u>?

12. Does Bowden's <u>Dictionary of American Religious Biography</u> have a subject index?

Now read the preface to Adam's <u>A Reader's Guide to the Great Religions</u>. Note the difference in structure. While Slavens and Wilson was a two part work, Adam's work has thirteen bibliographic essays which contain references to resources, but without individual annotations. Using the subject index at the back of the volume find a reference tool which focuses on each of the following subjects:

Hittite Mythology

The Aeneid

The early history of the Aztec people

The mythology of the Chinese

Cargo movement

A Primer on Theological Research Tools

James Fraser's method of research

Christian Gnosticism

The Duke of Chou

The Day of Atonement

Peyote Cult

Celtic Epic tradition

Christian Mysticism

Dualism

Neo-Positivism

Muslim piety

The role of the pilgrimage in the Sikh Religion

Now use the index of author, compilers, translators, and editors to answer the following questions.

13. For whom did Khazan Singh work?

14. Which work is more current: Guttmann's, <u>Philosophies of Judaism</u>, or Husik's, <u>A History of Medieval Philosophy</u>?

15. In what year was C.H. Dodd's <u>The Apostolic Preaching</u> published?

16. What was the name of Kenneth Cragg's important work on the Quran and when was it published?

Cyril Barber's <u>The Minister's Library</u> has a much narrower scope and different aims than the other volumes. Read the introduction in order to ascertain the scope and goals of Barber's work. Notice that it concludes with a subject index, an author index, and a title index. Using these indices, answer the following questions:

17. Who was the author of <u>How to Live Through Junior High School</u>?

18. What call number is recommended for Wesner Fallow's <u>The Modern Parent and the Teaching Church</u>?

19. Who was the publisher of Ironside's <u>Except Ye Repent</u>?

20. Has J.N.D. Kelly ever written a commentary on the Epistles of Peter?

21. What was the original language and the date of publication of Frederick Godet's <u>Commentary on the Gospel of John</u>?

LESSON 2- GENERAL REFERENCE TOOLS II

Cross, F.L. and E.A. Livingstone, eds. The Oxford
   Dictionary of the Christian Church. 2d. ed. London:
   Oxford University Press, 1974.

The Oxford Dictionary of the Christian Church, first
edited under F.L. Cross, Lady Margaret Professor of
Divinity at the University of Oxford from 1944-68, and
continued under Miss E.A. Livingstone, is one of the most
significant reference tools in theological studies. It
has a broad range and depth of coverage that is
informative to both the beginner and specialist.

Begin your perusal of this tool by reading its preface
and try to gain the reasons for the publication, the
strengths and weaknesses of the volume, and its scope of
coverage. Read both the current preface and the lengthy
preface to the first edition. Look at the list of
contributors following the preface. Following this list
are the abbreviations used in the volume. Following a
biographical essay on Frank Lesley Cross are the entries
of the dictionary in alphabetical order.

In order to appreciate the range of this volume read the
entries for Binding and Loosing, Cotta, Flags on Church
Towers, Karl Heim, St. Leonard, Patmos, Cope, Gifford
Lectures, Oxford Movement, Doctors of the Church, Humanae
Vitae, Casuistry, and 'Ain Karim.

An important class of entries in this Oxford Dictionary
is the biographical entry. Turn to the entry for
Augustine of Hippo. Read the entry and see the level of
treatment given. Also, look to see if there are cross
references to other articles. Following the article, in
smaller print, is the bibliography, a valuable feature
of this dictionary. Notice that the first paragraph
contains works of St. Augustine, the dates of their
composition, and the volumes in Migne's Patrologia Latina
in which the works are located (Patrologia Latina is
abbreviated PL). The second paragraph lists collected
works of Augustine beginning with the 1506 edition and

the critical editions which are appearing in the various modern updates. The next paragraph covers translations of his writings citing the Library of the Fathers and the Nicene and Post-Nicene Fathers and various volumes in a current series, The Fathers of the Church. The next paragraph deals with biographies about Augustine, beginning with that of Possidius, his friend and disciple, and moving through the biography by Mandouze, published in Paris in 1968. The concluding paragraphs contain various studies on Augustine's theology and studies on individual works.

Turn to the entry on Chrysostom and answer the following questions:

1.   Are Chrysostom's works contained in Migne's Patrologia Latina?

2.   How many volumes are in Field's edition of Chrysostom's Homilies on Matthew?

3.   Which volumes of the Nicene and Post-Nicene Fathers of the Church contain English translations o Chrysostom's works?

4.   Who wrote the early biography of Chrysostom entitled Dialogus de Vita St. Joannis Chrysostomi?

5.   Which sections of Sozoman's Church History cover the life of Chrysostom?

6. Which years were the two volumes Chrysostomus Baur's biography of Chrysostom issued in German and in English?

Answer the following questions to get a picture of the range of the Oxford Dictionary.

7. How many synods were held at Arles?

8. Are bishops in the Armenian Church usually married or celibate?

9. How did the name Huguenots arise?

10. In what year did J.B. Lightfoot become Bishop of Durham?

11. Who was Peter the Chanter?

12. What are the differences between Regular Canons and Regular Clerks?

13. What was the earliest council held in the Spanish Church?

14. What part of the ecclesiastical garb of a literate priest in the Church of England distinguishes his status?

9

15. Where is the Nitrian desert?

16. What nationality was St. Ninian?

17. Did Nikon the Patriarch of Moscow die in office?

18. Who is the Dean of the Arches in the Church of England?

19. What are the 7 deadly sins?

20. Of what order was St. Francis Borgia a member?

21. What order did St. John Bosco found?

22. In what year was the Osservatore Romano founded?

LESSON 3- GENERAL REFERENCE TOOLS III

Read the prefaces and introductions to the reference tools listed below. Note the dates of publication, the editors, the scope of the work and whether the articles are signed (listing their authors) or unsigned. Note if there is a list of contributors in the front of the volume and if there are bibliographies with every article, some articles, and the extent of the bibliographies. Also check to see if there are indices and other aids contained in these reference tools.

Douglas, J.D. ed., The New International Dictionary of the Christian Church. Grand Rapids: Zondervan, 1978.

Eliade, Mircea. ed., The Encyclopedia of Religion, 16 vols. New York: Macmillan, 1987.

Jackson, Samuel Macauley, et al., eds. The New Schaff-Herzog Encyclopedia of Religious Knowledge, 12 vols. New York: Funk and Wagnells, 1908. 12 vols. and vol 13 index. Grand Rapids: Baker Book House, 1949-50, 1954.

MacDonald, William J. et al., eds. New Catholic Encyclopedia, 15 vols. New York: McGraw-Hill, 1967. with supplements 1974, 1979.

Roth, Cecil, et al. eds. Encyclopedia Judaica, 16 vols. New York: Macmillan, 1972. Encyclopedia Judaica Yearbook. 1975-.

Attempt to answer each of the following questions in each of the reference tools above and list the tools in which you found an answer after each question.

1. Did Billy Sunday ever play professional baseball?

2. Find a biography of St. Augustine.

11

3.   In what year did Adolph Von Harnack die?

4.   In what year did John Calvin come to Geneva for the
     first time?

5.   Find an introduction to the Biblical book of Isaiah.

6.   Find an over-view of Arminianism.

7.   Find an over-view of Christianity in Iceland.

8.   Find a list of Popes.

9.   Find an article on the city of Jerusalem.

10. Find an article on abortion.

11. In what year was St. Ambrose born?

12. What are Christian views on Capitol Punishment?

After trying to answer each one of these questions in the reference tools covered in this unit evaluate each tool by the criteria of depth of coverage, intended scope of the work, currency of information and ease of use.

LESSON 4- BIBLICAL STUDIES

Bromiley, Goeffrey, ed. <u>International Standard Bible Encyclopedia</u>, 4 vols. Grand Rapids: Eerdmans, 1979.

Cheyne, T.K. and J.S. Black eds. <u>Encyclopedia Biblica</u> 4 vols. New York: Macmillan, 1899-1903.

<u>Interpreters Dictionary of the Bible</u>, 4 vols. New York: Abingdon, 1962. supplement v. 1976.

Orr, James ed. <u>International Standard Bible Encyclopedia</u>, 5 vols. Chicago: Severence, 1930.

Steinmueller, John E. and Kathryn Sullivan, eds. <u>Catholic Biblical Encyclopedia</u>, 2 vols. New York: Wagner, 1959.

Tenney, Merrill C. ed. <u>Zondervan Pictorial Encyclopedia of the Bible</u>, 5 vols. Grand Rapids: Zondervan, 1975.

Examine the reference tools listed above, reading the various prefaces and introductions, noting the dates of publication, authors, and whether the articles are signed. Also observe the goals and perspectives as noted in the preface, and the indices and supplements and various other aids to usage. Then use each of the reference tools to answer each of the questions below. After each question list the tools in which you found an answer.

1. Find an outline of the content of the book of Romans.

2. How far is it from Bethlehem to Nazareth?

3. Find a list of kings of the Northern Kingdom.

15

4.   Find a picture of the old city of Jerusalem.

5.   Find an article on Old Testament Chronology.

6.   Find a biography of King David.

7.   Read the various introductions to the book of
      Genesis and ascertain the positions of these
      introductions on the Creation-Evolution debate, and
      the debate over Mosaic authorship of the first five
      books of the Bible.

8.   Find a synthetic discussion of the various accounts
      of the life of Christ in the four Gospels.

9.   Find maps which illustrate the journeys of Paul
      contained in the book of Acts.

10.   Find maps which illustrate the division of the
      promised land among the tribes of Israel.

11.   Find an article on justification as a theme in
      Biblical Theology.

12.   Find an article on the Genesis flood.

13. Find a discussion of the chronological difficulties in the events narrated in the book of Judges.

After answering these questions in the various reference tools covered in this unit, please make some summary notes regarding the perspective and the level of coverage in each tool.

LESSON 5- BIBLICAL STUDIES II

Bauer, Johannes B. ed. Sacramentum Verbi: Encyclopedia of Biblical Theology, 3 vols. London: Sheed and Ward, 1970.

Brown, Colin, ed. New International Dictionary of New Testament Theology, 3 vols. Grand Rapids: Zondervan, 1975-1978.

Kittel, Gerhard, ed. Theological Dictionary of the New Testament, 10 vols. Grand Rapids: Eerdmans, 1964-76.

Leon-Dufour, Xavier, ed. Dictionary of Biblical Theology. 2d ed. rev. and enl. London: Chapman, 1973.

Use Bauer's Sacramentum Verbi: Encyclopedia of Biblical Theology, and Leon-Dufour's Dictionary of Biblical Theology, to answer each of the following questions.

1.   Find an article addressing faith as a subject of Biblical Theology.

2.   Find an article on Spiritual Gifts.

3.   Find an article on the biblical teaching of providence.

4.   Find an article on the Image of God in man.

5.   Find a signed article with a bibliography on war.

6.   Find an article on the servant of the Lord.

7.   Find an article on Messianism.

8.   Find an article on reconciliation.

9.   Find an article on the concept of law.

10. Find an article on the biblical concept of love.

11. Find an article on the biblical teaching of Baptism.

The next two sources reviewed in this unit, are the New International Dictionary of New Testament Theology and the Theological Dictionary of the New Testament. Using the indices of each of these works, read articles in each work on the following subjects:

Scripture

Gog and Magog

Resurrection

Faith

Knowledge

Spiritual Gifts

Tongues

Also, use the indices of these tools to find references to concepts in the following passages:

Ps 23

Mark 8:38

Phil 2:1

I Cor 8

Romans 12

LESSON 6- BIBLICAL STUDIES III

Aharoni, Yohanan, and Michael Avi-Yonah. <u>The Macmillan Bible Atlas</u>. rev. ed. New York: Macmillan, 1977.

Baly, Denis. <u>Geographical Companion to the Bible</u>. New York: McGraw-Hill, 1963.

<u>Encyclopedia of Archaeological Excavations in the Holy Land</u>, 4 vols. Englewood Cliffs, N.J.: Prentice-Hall, 1975-8.

Finegan, Jack. <u>Handbook of Biblical Chronology</u>. Princeton: Princeton University Press, 1964.

Grollenberg, Luc H. <u>Atlas of the Bible</u>. Paris: Elsevier, 1956.

May, Herbert G. ed. <u>Oxford Bible Atlas</u>. 2d ed. London: Oxford University Press, 1974.

Negenmann, Jan H. <u>New Atlas of the Bible</u>. Garden City, N.Y.: Doubleday, 1969.

Negev, Avraham. ed. <u>Archaeological Encyclopedia of the Holy Land</u>. New York: Putnam, 1972.

Rowley, H.H. <u>Dictionary of Bible Place Names</u>. Old Tappan, N.J.: Revell, 1970.

Wright, George Ernest and Floyd Vivian Filson. <u>The Westminster Historical Atlas to the Bible</u>. Philadelphia: Westminster Press, 1956.

A Primer on Theological Research Tools

Using the atlases listed below, answer all of the
following questions. Note the differing qualities of
indices in each atlas, the types of maps, their scale,
coloration, and how they are keyed to Scripture. Also
observe the use of general maps for a specific
geographical area and maps for individual events
mentioned in the biblical text. After the questions, list
each tool in which you found an answer.

The Westminster Historical Atlas of the Bible
Atlas of the Bible
New Atlas of the Bible
Oxford Bible Atlas
Macmillan Bible Atlas

1.   How far is it from Jerusalem to Nazareth?

2.   How far is it on an average, from the Jordan River
     to the Mediterranean Sea?

3.   What are the dimensions of the Sea of Galilee?

4.   What it the elevation of the Dead Sea?

5.   What is the elevation of Jerusalem?

6.   Find a map or maps portraying events in the Book of
     Judges.

7.   Find a map of Jerusalem in Christ's day?

8. Find a map of Jerusalem in the time of King David?

9. How far is it from the Land of Goshen to Kadesh Barnea?

10. How far is it from Jerusalem to Antioch-on-the-Orontes?

11. Did Paul visit Cyprus on his third missionary journey?

12. Where did Paul cross from Asia Minor into Europe?

13. How far is it from Philippi to Athens?

14. Find a map showing the route that Paul took on his trip from Jerusalem to Rome.

Having answered the above questions in all of the atlases of this unit, now attempt to answer each of the following questions in the atlas which will give the answer most efficiently.

15. Find a map showing the exploits of Jephthah in Judges 11.

16. Find a map showing the destruction of the Kingdom of Assyria by the Babylonians.

17. Find a map showing the location of the area of Egypt where the Jewish leaders of the revolt fled with Jeremiah after the assassination of the governor appointed by Nebuchadnezzar.

18. Find a map of Palestine as envisioned in the visions of Ezekiel.

19. Find a map of the campaigns of Alexander the Great.

20. Find a map showing the siege of Jerusalem by the Romans in AD 70.

21. Find a picture of a bust of Marc Anthony.

22. Find a map showing the mean annual rainfall in Palestine.

23. Find a map showing the vegetation of Palestine during biblical times.

24. Find a picture of a fragment of the limestone stelle of Pharaoh's Shishak at Megiddo.

25. Find a map detailing the expansion of Assyria.

26. Find a map showing the events recorded in the books of Samuel.

27. Find a map detailing the geographical context of the events of the books of the Maccabees.

28. Find maps comparing the territorial divisions of Palestine during the Maccabean period, the period under Herod the Great, under Herod Agrippa, and under Herod Agrippa II.

29. Find maps comparing the expansion of the Christian church during the times of Paul's ministry, the end of the second century, and the Council of Nicea.

30. Find a plan for the city of Jerusalem as it was restored after the exile.

31. Find a genealogical tree of Herod's family.

32. Find a pictorial reconstruction of the Synagogue at Capernaum.

Using the Encyclopedia of Archeological Excavations in the Holy Land answer the following questions:

33. What are the dates of the Iron Age, IA?

34. What are the dates of the Hasmonian period?

35. Who was the Byzantine Emperor in 531?

36. When was Nerva emperor of Rome?

37. What were the dates of Ramses I?

38. What were the dates of the first dynasty in Egypt?

39. When did Alexander Jannaeus, the Hasmonian King, reign?

Now read the articles on the following places to ascertain the types of information given in each entry.

Caesarea

Jerusalem

Beersheba

Masada

Hazor

Joppa

Read the entries for the same cities in the <u>Archeological Encyclopedia of the Holy Land</u> and compare the entries.

LESSON 7- HISTORICAL STUDIES

The various tools viewed in this unit serve as general introductions to Church History and as biographical sources to the lives of various Christian leaders.

Bowden, Henry Warner. Dictionary of American Religious Biography. Westport, Conn.: Greenwood, 1977.

Butler, Alban. Butler's Lives of the Saints, 4 vols. New York: Kenedy, 1963. 4v.

Delany, John J. Dictionary of Saints. New York: Doubleday, 1980.

Farmer, David Hugh. The Oxford Dictionary of Saints. Oxford: Clarendon Press, 1978.

Jedin, Hubert and J. Dolan, eds. History of the Church. New York: Seabury and Crosroad, 1965 9v.

Schaff, Philip. History of the Christian Church, 7 vols in 8. New York: Scribner. 1889-1910.

Please attempt to answer the following questions in each of the reference tools listed above. After each question list each tool in which you were able to find an answer to the question.

Questions:

1. In what year did St. Augustine write his confessions?

2. In what year did John Chrysostom die?

3. What years did John Calvin spend in Strassburg?

4. What were the events that led to Abelard's writing
    <u>The Story of My Calamities</u>?

5. Was John Cassian a proponent of Augustinian
    Theology?

6. Who was Pope when Martin Luther posted his 95
    thesis?

7. Who is the patron saint of librarians?

8. On what day is the Feast of St. John Chrysostom
    celebrated?

9. Who was Pope during the first Vatican Council?

10. In what years did the Council of Trent meet?

11. Did Philip Melanchthon and John Calvin ever exchange
    correspondence?

12. Summarize Anselm's views on the Atonement.

13. Who died earlier, Ignatius of Antioch, or John of Damascus?

Having attempted to answer each of these questions in the various reference tools covered in this unit, please note the perspectives of the different tools. Also note which tools give biographical access and the various degrees of helpfulness of the indices contained in each source.

LESSON 8- HISTORICAL STUDIES II

Anderson, Charles S. Augsburg Historical Atlas of
   Christianity in the Middle Ages and Reformation.
   Minneapolis: Augsburg, 1967.

Gaustad, Edwin Scott. Historical Atlas of Religion in
   America. Rev. ed. New York: Free Press, 1977.

Littell, Franklin H. The Macmillan Atlas History of
   Christianity. New York: Macmillan, 1976.

The three works reviewed in this unit are atlases
designed to aid one in the study of the history of
Christianity. Through the use of maps, charts, graphs,
and other pictorial representations, they seek to
illumine facts which otherwise might be difficult to
comprehend. Familiarize yourself with the scope, and
perspective of these atlases by reading their various
introductions and prefaces before attempting to answer
the questions in this unit.

Using Gaustad's Historical Atlas of Religion in America
answer the following questions:

1. Where were Anglican churches concentrated in the
    colonies in the 1750?

2. Where were Lutheran churches concentrated in the
    colonies in 1750?

3. How many Baptist churches were in America in 1820?

33

4. In 1850, were there more Methodist churches or Baptist churches in America?

5. In 1850, what percentage of people in the United States had been born in Ireland?

6. In what areas of the country were Roman Catholic churches concentrated in 1850?

7. In what area of the country were Universalist churches concentrated in 1850?

8. Where were the greatest concentrations of churches in the Church of the Nazarene in 1950?

9. Where were the greatest concentrations of Quaker Churches in 1850?

10. Where were the greatest concentrations of Methodist Churches in the U.S. in 1950?

11. What two states had the greatest concentrations of Mormons in 1906?

12. What three states had the greatest concentrations of Lutherans in 1906?

13. What state had the greatest concentration of Dutch people in 1790?

14. What percentage of the population in the U.S. was of English background in 1779?

15. What state had the greatest proportion of German people in 1790?

16. Did Roman Catholic Churches grow at a faster rate between 1730-40, or between 1670-80?

17. Were there any French Reformed Churches in the New England colonies in 1750?

18. In 1660, were there more Congregational or Anglican churches in the colonies?

Using Anderson's <u>Augsburg Historical Atlas of Christianity in the Middle Ages and Reformation</u> answer the following questions.

19. Was Erfurt a frontier trading station during the time of Charles the Great?

20. Did Islam spread to the area of modern Afghanistan before or after Mohammed's death?

21. During the time of Gregory the Great was the island of Cyprus in the Patriarchate of Antioch or the Patriarchate of Jerusalem?

22. When the Carolingian Empire was divided at the treaty of Verdon in 843, under whose control was Italy placed?

23. Did the Vikings ever establish a kingdom in southern Italy and Sicily?

24. At what university town did Gottschalk flourish?

25. Was there a university at Pisa in the 12th century?

26. During the reign of Gregory I, did the eastern Empire claim Rome?

27. What raw material did Scandinavia provide in medieval commerce and industry?

28. Was the church of San Sebastiano inside or outside the walls of Rome during the medieval period?

29. Where were the major areas of conflict during the Thirty Years War?

Use the <u>Macmillan Atlas History of Christianity</u> to answer the following questions:

30. According to tradition, where did the Apostle Thomas minister?

31. According to tradition, where did the Apostle Simon the Zealot minister?

32. Where was Marcion born?

33. Where did Montanus and his movement flourish?

34. Which wall at Constantinople encloses more area, the wall of Constantine, or the wall of Theodosius?

35. After the Council of Chalcedon in 451, where were the strongholds of Monophysite Christianity?

36. Where is Lindisfarne located?

37. Find a map showing how much of Britain was controlled by the Norseman during Alfred the Great's reign?

38. In the siege of Jerusalem in 1099, which portion of the wall was guarded by Jewish Militia?

39. Did the Mongolian Empire include the city of Kiev in 1275?

40. What year did the Black Death spread into England?

41. When were the Moors driven out of Grenada?

42. In what year was the University at Oxford founded?

43. Find a map showing areas of revival on the American frontier?

44. Find a map showing places where Karl Marx worked.

LESSON 9- THEOLOGICAL STUDIES

The sources reviewed in this unit are dictionaries and encyclopedias of theology written from a particular perspective. Please read the prefaces and introductions to these works and note the perspective, the list of authors, if the articles are signed, and the extent of bibliography contained in the articles.

Elwell, Walter A. ed. Evangelical Dictionary of Theology. Grand Rapids: Baker, 1984.

Rahner, Karl, ed. Encyclopedia of Theology: The Concise Sacramentum Mundi. New York: Seabury, 1975.

Rahner, Karl, ed. Sacramentum Mundi: An Encyclopedia of Theology, 6 vols. New York: Seabury 1968-70.

Richardson, Alan, ed. A Dictionary of Christian Theology. Philadelphia: Westminster Press, 1969.

Taylor, Richard S. ed. Beacon Dictionary of Theology. Kansas City: Beacon Hill Press, 1983.

Attempt to answer the following questions from each of the works listed above. After each question list the tools in which you were able to find an answer.

1.   What is predestination?

2.   What is evangelicalism?

3.   What are the theological concepts discussed in the book of Mark?

4.   What are theistic proofs for the existence of God?

5.   How should one view the attributes of God?

6.   Find an article on Eschatology.

7.   What is prophecy?

8.   What is entire-sanctification?

9.   Find an article on the gift of tongues.

10. Find an article on the sacraments.

11. What is the Christian view of baptism?

12. What is eternal security?

13. Find an article on church government.

14. What is meant by the Authority of Scripture?

15. What is meant by Inspiration?

After you have tried to answer the questions in each of the tools, evaluate each tool by the criteria of ease of use, range of coverage, point of view, level of treatment and other features such as cross-referencing.

LESSON 10- THEOLOGICAL STUDIES II

The works studied in this unit are supplemental sources
in the area of theology containing various pieces of
information often difficult to find but essential to
theological research.

Henry, Carl F. H. ed. Baker's Dictionary of Christian
    Ethics. Grand Rapids: Baker, 1973.

Childress, James F. and John Macquarrie, eds. The
    Westminister Dictionary of Christian Ethics.
    Philadelphia: Westminster Press, 1986.

Mead, Frank S. Handbook of Denominations in the United
    States. Nashville: Abingdon Press, 1975.

Piepkorn, Arthur Carl. Profiles in Belief: the
    religious bodies of the United States and Canada,
    4 vols. New York: Harper and Row, 1977-79.

Yearbook of American and Canadian Churches. Nashville:
    Abingdon Press, 1916-.

Using the Yearbook of American and Canadian Churches,
answer the following questions:

1. What is the headquarters address for the North
    American Baptist Conference?

2. Who are the officers of the Liberal Catholic Church
    Province of the U.S.A.?

3. Who was the founder of the Kodesh Church of
    Emmanuel?

43

4. When was the Elim Fellowship founded?

5. Does the United Holy Church of America Inc. practice foot washing?

6. Who is the current Archbishop of the Romanian Orthodox Church in America?

7. What is the name of the periodical published by the Presbyterian Church in Canada?

8. What is the address for the chief officer of the Duck River Association of Baptists?

9. What is the difference between the Church of God, Anderson, Indiana, and the Church of God, Cleveland, Tennessee?

10. Who is the president of the Berean Fundamental Churches?

11. What is the phone number for the Church of God Beacon?

12. What is the address of the Assembly of God Graduate School?

13. With what denomination is the School of Theology at Claremont associated?

Read the prefaces and introductory materials to the <u>Baker Dictionary of Christian Ethics</u>, and the <u>Dictionary of Christian Ethics</u> and then read the articles in both dictionaries on the following subjects.

Abortion

Alcoholism

Euthanasia

Adultery

Divorce

Environmental Pollution

Law and Gospel

Sodomy

Sports

Socialism

Stewardship

Sterilization

Birth Control and Marriage

Compare the scope and doctrinal perspective of the articles in the dictionaries. Also note which subjects are not covered in either dictionary.

Answer the following questions from Mead's, <u>Handbook of Denominations</u>:

14. Who was the founder of the Church of Christ Holiness U.S.A.?

15. When did the National Baptist Evangelical Life and Soul Saving Assembly of the U.S.A. become an independent body divorcing itself from the National Baptist Convention?

16. What are the four principles of Landmark Baptist?

17. What are the six principles of General Six Principle Baptists?

18. Who was the founder of the Two-Seed-In-The-Spirit Predestinarian Baptists?

19. Where were the Churches of the Living God founded?

20. What is the parent body of the House of God which is the Church of the Living God the Pillar and Ground of the Truth Incorporated?

21. Who are the Yorker Brethren?

22. What is another name for the Old German Baptist Brethren?

23. Who is the founder of the Apostolic Overcoming Holy Church of God?

24. When was the Apostolic Faith organized in Portland, Oregon?

Answer the following questions from Piepkorn's, <u>Profiles of Belief</u>. Notice that volumes 3, and 4 are bound together and the index for volume 3 is in the middle of the bound volume.

25. How did the Gospel Harvester Evangelistic Association get its name?

26. What is the address of the Alpha and Omega Christian Church?

27. In what year did the True Fellowship Pentecostal Church of America, Inc. withdraw from the Alpha and Omega Christian Church of America, Inc.?

28. What is the difference between the Church of God of the Mountain Assembly, Inc. and the Church of God of the Original Mountain Assembly, Inc.?

29. How many dispensations did Charles H. Welsh of the Prison Epistles Dispensational Groups believe in?

30. When was the American Mission for Open and Closed Churches, Inc. founded?

31. In what year did Rev. Viola Bankston found the Blessed Martin Spiritual Church in her kitchen with three other members?

32. Where did L.T. Nicholes of the Megiddo Mission Church go after he received a dispensation from combat from President Lincoln during the Civil War?

33. When was the Kingdom Truth Assembly of Irvington, New Jersey founded?

34. When was the first Church of the Estonian Orthodox Church in Exile founded in the U.S.?

35. When was the Conservative Congregational Christian Conference founded?

36. Where is the National Association of Free Will Baptist headquartered?

37. Who was the founder of the Schwenkfelder Church?

38. What are some doctrinal distinctives of the Russian
    Molokan Spiritual Christian?

LESSON 11- MINISTERIAL STUDIES

Please read the introductory materials in the sources
listed below and look at the end of each volume to see
the type of indices contained in each work.

Cully, Kendig B. ed. The Westminster Dictionary of
    Christian Education. Philadelphia: Westminster,
    1963.

Davies, John G. The New Westminster Dictionary of
    Liturgy and Worship. Philadelphia: Westminster,
    1986.

Julian, John, ed. Dictionary of Hymnology, 2 vols. New
    York: Dover, 1907.

McDormand, Thomas Bruce and Frederic S. Crossman.
    Judson Concordance to Hymns. Valley Forge, Pa.:
    Judson Press, 1965.

Spencer, Donald A. Hymn and Scripture Selection Guide.
    Valley Forge, Pa: Judson, 1977.

Turnbull, Ralph G. ed. Baker's Dictionary of Practical
    Theology. Grand Rapids: Baker, 1967.

Using the Baker Dictionary of Practical Theology, answer
the following questions:

1.   Find an article on the history of homiletics.

2.   Find an article on Roman Catholic preaching.

3.   Find an article on style in Puritan preaching.

4. Find an article on allegory as an issue in hermeneutics.

5. Find an article on contemporary sermonic style.

6. Find an article on counseling the bereaved.

7. Find an article on church administration from the Lutheran perspective.

8. Find an article on Reformation and Post-Reformation creeds.

9. Find an article on the pastor as a worship leader.

10. Find an article on medieval worship.

11. Find an article on tithing.

12. Find an article on organizing a Christian school.

Using the <u>Westminster Dictionary of Christian Education</u>, answer the following questions:

13. What is a laboratory school?

14. Find an article relating Neo-orthodox Theology to Christian Education.

15. Find an article on the history of Reformation Day.

16. Find an article on issues facing suburban churches.

17. Find an article on the use of men's groups in the local church.

18. What is idealism?

19. When did the state first take over responsibility for providing elementary education in England and Wales?

20. What is pragmatism?

Use the The New Westminister Dictionary of Liturgy and Worship to answer the following questions:

21. What is the earliest reference to the sign of the cross?

22. What is the origin of the English word lent?

23. Find an exposition of the Jehovah's Witness view of marriage.

24. What is a pall?

25. What is genuflexion?

26. Why is it customary to face eastward during worship?

Answer the following questions using the Judson Concordance to Hymns:

27. What is the correct title of a hymn that has the line, "Against me, earth and hell combined"?

28. What is the correct title of the hymn with the line, "Come to Bethlehem and see"?

29. Which hymn contains the following line: "Swift to its close, ebbs out life's little day"?

Answer the following questions form the Hymn and Scripture Selection Guide:

30. Find a hymn which deals with the events in the book of Ruth, chapter 2.

31. Find a hymn which could be used when preaching on the parables in Matthew 13.

32. Find a hymn which can be used when preaching on the Great Commission from Matthew 28.

33. Find hymns which would be appropriate with the book of Third John.

34. Which Scriptures would be appropriate to use with the hymn "Christ the Lord is Risen Today"?

35. Which Scriptures would be most appropriate with the hymn "I Love to tell the Story"?

Use Julian's _Dictionary of Hymnology_ to answer the following questions:

36. When did the hymn "All Hail the Power of Jesus Name" first appear in print?

37. What is a breviary?

38. Are there any hymns sung today that are attributed to Ambrose, Bishop of Milan in the 4th century?

39.   Find   a   list   of   American   hymnals   showing   what
      proportion   of   the   hymns   contained   in   them   are   of
      American origin.

40.   Find   a   listing   of   the   hymns   written   by   Francis
      Havergal.

41.   What is a missal?

LESSON 12- WORLD MISSION AND COMPARATIVE RELIGION

Brandon, S.G.F. ed. Dictionary of Comparative Religion.
    New York: Scribner's, 1970.

Bulfinch's Mythology. New York: Crowell.

Coxil, H. Wakelin and Kenneth Grubb, eds. World Christian
    Handbook. London: World Dominion Press, 1968.

Neill, Stephen, Gerald H. Anderson and John Goodwin, eds.
    Concise Dictionary of the Christian World Mission.
    Nashville: Abingdon Press, 1971.

Parrinder, Geoffrey. A Dictionary of Non-Christian
    Religions. Philadelphia: Westminster Press, 1971.

World Christian Encyclopedia. Oxford: Oxford University
    Press, 1982.

Read the prefaces and look at the various indices and
other finding aids in the reference tools listed above.

Use the World Christian Handbook to answer the following
questions:

1.   List the Bible Societies that are active in Greece.

2.   In which African countries is the American Bible
      Society working?

3.   At the time of the publication of this reference
      tool, how many ordained, national workers were in
      Angola?

4. At the time of the publication of this handbook, what were the number of communicant members of the Assemblies of God in Poland?

5. At the time of the writing of this book, were there more Baptists or Seventh Day Adventists in Romania?

6. Find the address for Fact and Faith Films in London.

7. Find the address for the headquarters of the YMCA in Norway.

8. Find the address for the Methodist Church in North Africa, headquartered in Algeria.

Use the Concise Dictionary of the Christian World Mission to answer the following questions:

9. In what year was Charles Henry Brent born?

10. What languages did Henry Martyn work in during his mission work with William Carey?

11. When were the Maryknoll Fathers founded?

12. What is the current name for what was formally called the Society for the Propagation of the Gospel in Foreign Parts?

13. When was the Society for Promoting Christian Knowledge founded?

14. What is the Theological Education Fund?

Answer the following questions from Bulfinch's Mythology:

15. In the Arthurian legends, who built the Round Table?

16. According to legend, which city in England was founded by King Lear?

17. Who were the Druids and what role in society did they perform?

18. How far is the Isle of Iona from the Scottish mainland?

19. Who were the Skalds in Teutonic Mythology?

20. What are Runes?

21. In Nordic Mythology were the elves favorably disposed towards men or their enemies?

22. Who was Balder in Scandinavian Mythology?

23. What were Scylla and Charybdis?

Use <u>A Dictionary of Non-Christian Religions</u> to answer the following questions:

24. When did the Jewish Rabbi Abbaye live?

25. Who built the Maze called Labyrinth?

26. In Islam, who are the Jinn?

27. In Hindu religious ceremonies, what is Ghee?

28. In what year did Gobind Singh, the 10th Guru of the Sikhs die?

Use the <u>Dictionary of Comparative Religion</u> to answer the following questions:

29. What was the Bartholomew Day's Massacre?

30. What does the word Hades mean?

31. What is the I Ching?

32. Which religions have a concept of pilgrimage?

Use the World Christian Encyclopedia to answer the following questions:

33. What is the dominant faith in Barbados?

34. What percentage of the people of Bangladesh are Christian?

35. Are there more professing Christians or Muslims in Bulgaria?

36. Is the Roman Catholic Church expected to grow in Gibraltar between 1900 and the year 2000?

37. What is the official State Church of Iceland?

38. Are the Christian churches expected to grow in Indonesia between now and the year 2000?

39. What percentage of the people of Mongolia are Christian?

40. What percentage of the people of Tonga are Protestant?

41. What is the address of the All India Prayer Fellowship?

42. What is the address for the Center For the Study of
     the Future, a research center in the U.S.?

LESSON 13- BIBLIOGRAPHIC TOOLS

The following questions have been selected to illustrate the uses and idiosyncrasies of <u>Books in Print</u> and its companion work, <u>Subject Guide to Books in Print</u>. These tools are the basic guides to what is available from the American publishing industry.

1.   Find books dealing with the concept of Biblical Law.

2.   Who is the publisher of <u>A Pictorial Bible Atlas</u> by E.M. Blaiklock?

3.   Who is the editor of <u>Ancient Near East in Pictures with Supplement</u>, and what is the most current edition?

4.   Find books on Biblical Higher Criticism.

5.   Find books on Muslim Art.

6.   How many introductions to the Gospels are currently in print?

7.   Are there any introductory texts in print which deal only with the Apocrypha?

8. How many Interlinear New Testaments are in print?

9. Are there any books in print dealing with the history of church and state relations?

10. Under what subject heading are books dealing with church and state from a Jewish perspective listed?

11. Are there any books recently published in print on church and state in Greece?

12. How many collections of Christmas sermons are in print?

13. Has Rosemary Ruether written works on the subject of Christianity and Progress which are still in print?

14. Are there any books in print on the subject of Christian Psychology from a Greek Orthodox perspective?

15. Find books on Christian evidences.

16. Under what subject headings can you find books on the subject of death?

17. Has Sydney Ahlstrom written a book on religion in the United States which is still in print?

18. Is Janet Fishburn's book on the social gospel still in print?

20. Find books on medical missions.

21. Find books on natural religion.

22. Find books on the subject of church polity.

23. How many books authored by F.F. Bruce are currently in print?

24. What is the address for the publisher Sposs, Inc.?

25. What is the telephone number of the Baker Book House?

26. Does one address orders to the Oxford University Press to the Madison Ave, New York address?

27. How many editions of Augustine's <u>Confessions</u> are still in print?

28. Has I. Howard Marshall written a commentary on Romans that is currently in print?

29. What is the cost of the cheapest available edition of Calvin's <u>Institutes</u>?

30. Is <u>Miracles and the Critical Mind</u> still in print and, if so, who is the author?

31. How many works by J.R.R. Tolkien are currently in print?

32. What is the latest edition of the <u>Oxford Dictionary of the Christian Church</u>?

33. Is Luther's commentary on Galatians in print and, if so, who is the publisher?

LESSON 14- BIBLIOGRAPHIC TOOLS II-INDICES AND ABSTRACTS

The indices listed below are used to find bibliographic citations.   As you look at the prefaces and the introductory materials of a recent edition of each index, please note the ones in which the abstracts are signed, those containing only abstracts, those containing no abstracts at all or selected abstracts, those containing book reviews, and the number of journals covered in each tool.

<u>Christian Periodical Index</u>.   Buffalo: Association of Christian Librarians, 1956-.

<u>Elenchus Bibliographicus Biblicus</u>. Louvain: Universitas Catholica Lovaniensis, 1924-.

<u>Index to Jewish Periodicals</u>. Cleveland: College of Jewish Studies Press, 1963-.

<u>Index to Religious Periodical Literature</u>.   Chicago: American Theological Library Association, 1953-1977. 12 v. continued as <u>Religion Index One: Periodicals</u>. 1978-.

<u>New Testament Abstracts</u>. Cambridge, Mass.: Weston School of Theology, 1956- v.1-.

<u>Old Testament Abstracts</u>. Washington: Catholic University of America, 1978-. v. 1-.

<u>Religious and Theological Abstracts</u>.   Myerstown, PA: Religious and Theological Abstracts, Inc., 1958-. v. 1-.

A Primer on Theological Research Tools

After reading the introductory materials to the latest issue of the indices listed above, use each to attempt to find resources on the following subjects. After each subject list the tools in which you were able to find appropriate citations and the subject headings where the information was found.

Paul's use of the Old Testament in II Corinthians

The Theology of Matthew

The Theology of John Calvin

Theological Education in America

Bible College education

The Theology of the Books of Moses

Evangelicalism in America in the 20th century

Medieval Theology

Compare the amount of resources found on each subject in the indices and compare the types of material indexed in each resource.

Answer the following questions using the most appropriate index or abstract:

1. Find a citation of a recent article on the book of Hebrews in English with an abstract.

2. Find the location of articles on the book of Galatians that deal with the theology of the Apostle Paul as contained in this book.

3. Find citations of articles on the subject of Biblical Theology with abstracts.

4. Find abstracts of books on the Pentateuch.

5. Find the location of resources dealing with Judges, chapter one.

6. Find citations of resources with abstracts on the Inter-Testamental period.

7. Is the <u>Jewish Journal of Sociology</u> indexed in the <u>Index to Jewish Periodicals</u>?

8. Find citations of articles about King Ahasuerus.

9. Find the location of an article about coins in ancient Israel.

10. Is the <u>American Journal of Archeology</u> indexed in <u>Elenchus Bibliographicus Biblicus</u>

11. Find citations of journal articles in English on the parables of Jesus in Matthew 13.

12. Find citations of articles in a variety of modern languages on New Testament Moral Theology.

13. Find citations of articles on the Nag Hammadi Texts.

14. Find citations of articles on methodology in the science of Archeology.

15. Locate an article written in <u>Christianity Today</u> in 1984, by Vernon Grounds, on the L'Abri Fellowship in Switzerland.

16. Find the citation of an article on the Laity by David Hall, written in 1984, with an abstract.

17. Find the location of an article entitled "Student Research at United Theological College", written in 1982.

18. Find the location of a review of F.F. Bruce's commentary on I and II Thessalonians, (published by Word in 1982).

19. Did W.H.C. Frend write a review of Peter Brown's, Society and the Holy in Late Antiquity, in 1983?

20. Was David Hubbard's book, Parables Jesus Told, published by Inter Varsity Press in 1981, reviewed in the Journal of Evangelical Theology?

21. List journals indexed in Christian Periodical Index but not in Religion Index One.

22. Find the citation of a recent article on a philosophy of education for Bible Colleges.

23. Find abstracts of journal articles written recently on Medieval Theology.

24. Are there journals abstracted in Religious and Theological Abstracts which are not indexed in Religion Index One?

25. Was Lane A. Scott writing abstracts for Religious and Theological Abstracts in 1984?

26. Where does Everett Furgason who writes abstracts for Religious and Theological Abstracts teach?